AFRICA'S DEMOCRATIC
DESPOT AND ITS TRANSITION

SULYMAN ABAYA

authorHOUSE®

AuthorHouse™ UK
1663 Liberty Drive
Bloomington, IN 47403 USA
www.authorhouse.co.uk
Phone: 0800 047 8203 (Domestic TFN)
       +44 1908 723714 (International)

© 2020 Sulyman Abaya. All rights reserved.

No part of this book may be reproduced, stored in a retrieval system, or transmitted by any means without the written permission of the author.

Published by AuthorHouse 02/22/2020

ISBN: 978-1-5462-8250-1 (sc)
ISBN: 978-1-5462-8249-5 (e)

Print information available on the last page.

Any people depicted in stock imagery provided by Thinkstock are models, and such images are being used for illustrative purposes only.
Certain stock imagery © Thinkstock.

This book is printed on acid-free paper.

Because of the dynamic nature of the Internet, any web addresses or links contained in this book may have changed since publication and may no longer be valid. The views expressed in this work are solely those of the author and do not necessarily reflect the views of the publisher, and the publisher hereby disclaims any responsibility for them.

Dedicated To:
Sir James Sunday Bamigboye, SAN:
A Forensic Advocate Extra-Ordinaire

ACKNOWLEDGMENTS

1. I thank Almighty God who provided me the wherewithal for the writing of this play. However, it wouldn't have been so possible without the hindsight, inspiration, ideas and staunch support of the people who provoked remote impetus and immediate antidotes to oppressive and undemocratic practices typified by 27th August, 2019. My appreciation goes to the following people:

2. (a) The traditional custodian of the locale which provided a miniature setting, His Eminence, Dr. (Alh) Ibrahim Sulu-Gambari, The Emir of Ilorin, Nigeria.

   (b) The "gathering stormers" who supported the ideas behind the work, Mr. Yusuf Alli (Managing Editor, The Nation), Mr. Lanre Abaya, Atlanta Georgia, The USA, Helon Habila (2001 Caine Prize Winner in Literature), Professor Bayo Lawal, Mr. Bayour Isaiah, Dr. (Mrs) Balqis Baraje and Barr. Hammed Olatunji Abaya.

3. Foremostly, my deep gratitude goes to an Avant-garde Legal Colossus and Bar Leader, Rev. John Olushola Baiyeshea, SAN. No less appreciated are Mr. Dayo Akinlaja, SAN and Dr. D.A. Ariyoosu.

4. My special gratitude also goes to the great Advocates of rule of law and champion of 27th August, 2019, namely: Mr. Mohammed Idowu Akande, Mr. Omotayo Ishola, Y.A. Alajo Esq., late Mrs. Omolara Adetutu Aluko (nee Adeyemi) who unfortunately died whilst this work went to print, Alh. Usman Mohammed Apalando and O.D. Jimoh Esq. In fact, my depth of gratitude cannot be adequate unless I recognize the following musketeers, late Mr. Abdulwahab Bamidele, Abiodun Dada Esq., Chief R.O. Balogun, Dr. Hussein Sadam Folohunso, Ismaila Raheem, Esq., Surajudeen Tijani, Esq. Ibn Mahmmud, A.S. Oseni, Esq., A.S. Abdullateef, Esq., Y.Y. Ajibade, Esq., S.U. Araga, Esq., L.O. Bello, Esq., G.T. Oniyo, A.L. Abdullahi Esq., Malik Abdulmajeed Esq., A.T. Yusuf, Esq., A.J. Edun, Esq., Shuaib Ibrahim Esq., A.R. Sheu, Esq., B.L. Shafi, Esq., S.T. Yahaya, Esq., J.S. Mohammed Esq., G.O. Osagbemi, Esq., Y.A. Usman, Esq., Rotimi Oyegbola, Esq., Alamayo Sulaiman Esq., Toafiq Alubarika, Esq., Lanre Yahya, Esq., A.E. Raji (Mrs), Oluwabunmi Joye (Mrs), M.A. Yusuf, Esq., B.A. Oni Esq., Y.A. Usman (Al-rohees) Mr. Kayode Adeoti, Alh Hakeem Garba, Mr. Funsho Abaskarara and Mr. Ibrahim Alege.

5. My special thanks goes to an extra-ordinary legal juggernaut and humanist, Mall. Yusuf O. Ali, SAN.

6. I equally acknowledge the contribution of the following personalities for their invaluable support; Alh. Ahmed Abaya, Alh. Yusuf Alabi Abaya, Alh. Modibo Sulu-Gambari, Alh. (Barr) H.O. Buhari, Chief Teju Oguntoye,

Alh. Nurudeen Funsho Abdullahi Adana, Mr. Ogunwale Tunji Gabriel, Alh. Babatunde Ajala, Magaji Araromi Community, Aremu Sheu, Esq., Alh. Abubakar Gatta, Mr. Hassan Kazeem, Alh. Umar Adelodun (Galadima Ngeri), Mallam AbdulGaniyu Abdulhameed and all the members of the Nigeria Bar Association Ilorin, Kwara State and all others too numerous to mention.

7. I appreciate in no small measure my publishers, AuthorHouseUK, for painstakingly making this play a quality product for international audience.

8. My thanks also goes to all my siblings, immediate and extended for their prayers and good wishes.

9. And lastly, my wife, Mrs. Aminat Abaya for her support and encouragement and my children for their endurance.

Sulyman Abaya
sulymanabaya@yahoo.com

CHARACTERS/DRAMATIS PERSONAE

1. **GENERAL ABU ILYASU** — Military Head of State and Commander-In-Chief of the Armed Forces of the Federal Republic of Nuaga.
2. **DR. CHUKWUMA** — Minister of Information
3. **MAJOR ADABA** — Commander of General Operations.
4. **SENATOR MICHAEL WOOD** — Chairman, Senate Committee on International Diplomacy and Democracy
5. **ORACLE OF NUAGA** — Eye & Mouth of the Federal Republic of Nuaga
6. **CHIEF ABIKA** — The Politician

ACT 1

SCENE 1

The State House. Generd Ilyasu and Dr. Chukuma engage in tetea-tete of the State's matters.

GENERAL ABU ILUASU: (Low voice) Dr. Chukwuma!
DR. CHUKWUMA: At your command, Your Excellency.
I remain your most faithful servant.
GENERAL ABU ILYASU: It will be when the world is over.
Then can I doubt your loyalty, of all the people, Dr. and by then my government as Head of State of Nuaga and Commander-in-Chief of the Armed Forces of Nuaga would have been over.
DR. CHUKWUMA: The world will not end, I pray
GENERAL ABU ILYASU: (With fervent prayer-fullness) Amen.
Dr. Chukwuma, I do always pray too.

That this doom to come be a mirage after all. The taste of power taught me this. And I imagine how sweet the former colonial masters had wielded and enjoyed power before finally relinquishing it to the natives over seven decades ago. But since my military progenitors had the opportunity to dispense with their might to oscillate power and authority to their side from the puppets those masters installed, I cannot help thanking God.
Nobody to blame, you know. Might is right.

DR. CHUKWUMA: Really really....Your Excellency.

GENERAL ILYASU: But one funny thing, Dr., confounding my ears to this day is untoward criticism by people that I call jealous forlorns and envious feebles among Nuagas and some powers abroad, blaming poverty, war and illiteracy as keeping Nuaga underdeveloped are products of our presence in the reign of power.

DR. CHUKWUMA: Your Excellency, don't be bothered... As a government no one in the whole world altogether attracts enemy than you do. Foes, detractors and countless ill-will people will dare to bring down your government. But can they in reality extirpate indomitable army in possession of guns?

GENERAL ILYASU: The gun is not even the point, though we have it. As a corrective government, we came to power simple to prepare New Dawn and New World. To rescue a land deeply sank into the mess put it. However, different verbiages rent the air; "An aberration". "A Bastard in the Seat of Power", "Undemocratic Government..."

DR. CHUKWUMA: You can't be bugged, Your Excellency

GENERAL ILYASU: Bugged. Dr? After all we have the gun.

DR. CHUKWUMA: Sir, I do as well hear Radicals, Democrats and the West are planning to close the page of Your Excellency's

GENERAL ILYASU: government. And open another, Democracy.

Let them.... Let them plot, plan scheme and all that, it is not their first time and may not be their last. All amount to forlorn ranting. As far as I know...

DR. CHUKWUMA: (Cuts in) it is a place you rightly occupy, General.

GENERAL ILYASU: Ofcourse it is my birthright. Something of heritage. A kind of filial possession. I shall be a bastard to disown the heritage of my predecessors even though they dash out intermittent cessation to cleverly put ephemeral smile on clamourers of that alien thing called Democracy. Democracy is alien to Nuaga, you know? (Blast from the door's ring buzz in) Let that Goddamn come in right away (Major Adaba enters, take a servile salute)

MAJOR ADABA: Sir, an American senator is leading a delegation. To make good their country earlier promise to enter into a discussion with you.

GENERAL ILYASU: Lead them into the Reception Room.
Their visit cannot hurry me to wind up a more important discussion. They either wait or leave. Whichever one they choose!.

MAJOR ADABA: Very well, sir (Takes another salute and leaves).

GENERAL ILYASU: Sheer intrusion and invasion. I can pre-empt those scoundrel motives.

DR. CHUKWUMA: Intrusion and invasion, really, Your Excellency. Successive raids on the land of Nuaga by these foreigners of a people since creation has got to stop. First slave trade, then colonialism. Now, another invasion …

GENERAL ILYASU: Not while I am in power. And in firm control too. Infact we have to gird our belt for a greater task.

DR. CHUKWUMA: From the day I got my letter of appointment as Your Excellency's Minister of Information I know, I have to sacrifice my life in the alter of your service.

GENERAL ILYASU: I couldn't have appointed somebody else for that post other than you, Dr. I can't see anybody that can contest your credentials. Talk of oration, persuasion, intelligence, knowledge ….

DR. CHUKWUMA: it was all by your grace, Sir.

GENERAL ILYASU: Even as I realize, you are the best of stuff of adviser, confidant and man for that matter.

DR. CHUKWUMA: Only by your mercy…, General.

GENERAL ILYASU: Dr. do you know I am a god, sort of? You understand what I mean?

DR. CHUKWUMA: I know, of course

GENERAL ILYASU: How do you understand it?

DR. CHUKWUMA: I know you are a god living in yesterday. Living in today. And living in tomorrow.

GENERAL ILYASU: (Enchantly shocked) Be straight to the point (with anxious curiosity) I mean… Mmm…say it straight and clear?

DR. CHUKWUMA: A god that will forever remain the pilot of the ship of Nuaga. In perpetuity

GENERAL ILYASU:	(with frenzy ecstasy) Truly, you have a very sound savvy, Dr.
DR. CHUKWUMA:	I can't be less, Your Excellency.
GENERAL ILYASU:	However, this is an Agenda.
DR. CHUKWUMA:	(Cuts in) which must be kept secret.
GENERAL ILYASU:	Summarily meaning…
DR. CHUKWUMA:	Hidden Agenda.
GENERAL:	Dr. you are a wizard, wallai. I have never seen a wit. By the way the Agenda goes like this: method of tactical trickery would be employed; strategy of deceit by which the whole world would be hushed and blindfolded by a transition that will never be; our programmes will sprawl on papers but nothing shall come out of it and you particularly will jingle false news and information about all our plans as to handing over quarters?
DR. CHUKWUMA:	I swear to God. These things will be kept secret, I promise. I remain your most faithful, loyal servile, and sincere servant, General.

SCENE 2

THE RECEPTION ROOM: General Ilyasu and Dr. Chukwuma exchange greetings with Senator Wood and the delegation and settle down to their seats

SENATOR WOOD: We thank you for the warmth reception accorded us. On behalf of Mr. Christopher Boston, the president of America and the people of United States we bring you great tidings. We bring the people of Nuaga happy tidings as well. Sir, as you may not be unaware that a revolution is sweeping across the whole world of a crusade for the reign of democracy all around the globe. This crusade, as you know, is a brain-child of the people of America to bring about a new world devoid of oppression and suppression but a world where peace, harmony and tranquility will prevail by accommodating free-will, majority rule and general consensus. This, everybody knows rests in the way the people are governed. (General and Dr. nod countlessly). Our country has been spearheading this project as a matter of international relations and diplomatic policy by entering into what I call bilateral agreement, United State on one hand, the rest of world, on the other.

This, the former Great Power, soviet Union recently acceded to though with a pint of salt by which the revolution swept that communism die-hard. Persistently we endeavour to let this wave cruise across Nuaga as well. But it has been the most stone-headed. The final lap of the project has come. This century must witness the end of military rule. Nuaga must embrace

GENERAL: democracy for the good of a peaceful world. That is the massage of our mission. (General cough for a breather. Gently sighs)
I thank your country for its crusade, more vigorously now pursued of which we are not at all unsupportive. And which we area also prepared and pray to embrace. But as much as we genufledge in soundry prayer, circumstance of our culture and heritage necessitate that things must always go bad and wrong. So that we always intervene in its governance to bring it back to normalcy. (Pause). However no land… No land in the face of this earth, I say is now thoroughly prepared as we are. To return Nuaga to democracy, its transition is what I have been discussing with Dr. Chukwuma. (Looks Dr. in the face who nods in reply) just before you arrived, to convey the genuine intention of this government

	to the people of Nuaga and the whole world. All machinery have been put in motion all structures in places.
SENATOR WOOD:	Sir, but Nuaga has always had transition sang and sand over and over without… handling-over.
GENERAL:	That you think it turns to cliché of ruse?
SENATOR WOOD:	Exactly.
GENERAL:	But senator, ours is a different case, most genuine and good intentioned. To buttress this point, let me share with you this anecdote of a sacred dream I had a night before the last. I have not told it to any man on earth.
	I saw God in plain white cloth appeared to me. He said: "The baton?" then I asked: "which baton?. He replied: "The baton of power, the time is now that you must give it to the people. For them to decide who holds it. It will never be handled by any man in khaki any more" (Ransack his brain for some re-collection) Mmm…He said

	lastly: "white men shall come to effect my order and will" (Delegation looks bewildered at this, taken aback). The matter is metaphysical. The God Almighty has a hand in our Transition to Democracy.
GENERAL:	Dr. Chukwuma, Please confirm my lies in this transition thing?
SENATOR WOOD:	Oh such thing, Sir. How can you tell lies, I don't doubt….
GENERAL:	No, let him bring out any ruse in my statement. Please Dr. speak…
DR. CHUKWUMA:	His Excellency had by Al-qurian in my presence and in the face of many many others not one time. Not twice. And sworn to it with the heaviest of imprecation to fall on his head if he does not make good his pledge.
SENATOR WOOD:	No iota of doubt sir…
GENERAL:	No let him speak it all.
DR. CHUKWUMA	About 1000,000,000.00 cuta has been earmarked for the programme. General mobilization of all Nuaga on Transition (GMNT);

	Transition Awareness Crusade (TAC), Committee of Wise men on Democracy (CMD) and some others have been set up and working round the clock…
	Personally, I don't mind wasting all saliva in my mouth. That will last me for a lifetime to wake Nuaga, from its slumber, if any, on to this.
SENATOR WOOD:	It is all well. Thank you very much for the homely reception and warmly talk. We will communicate your ardent sincerity in respect of the matter to our president and the people of America. (Delegation leaves. General and Dr. remain in the same room)
GENERAL:	Selfish lots, Dr.!
DR. CHUKWUMA:	I have never seen a more self-centered group of people!
GENERAL:	America! Mmm… That arrogant and disgruntled cheat parading herself as fore-runner and pace-setter of democracy.

DR. CHUKWUMA: General, she can arrogate the power to dictate rhythm and pulse of every nation. And we can afford to lie to the end.

GENERAL: Surely, it will serve them right. Forget their antics. Tomorrow we see for more auspicious business, Dr. Bye bye.

DR. CHUKWUMA: Good day, Your Excellency.

ACT 2

SCENE 1

THE STATE HOUSE: Exclusive meeting of Nuaga's Ruling Council in progress over which General Ilyasu presides. Oracle bursts in, having beaten official protocol.

ORACLE: Ruler of Nuaga! Commanders of Nuaga! Be not surprise. You are not seeing a wayfarer. Neither are you seeing a way warder. I am simply the God-sent Oracle of this land. Commissioned to bear the Eye and Mouth of this great part of the world, I come in variant eyes and mouth-the mosques, the churches etall. Nuaga we know is long sick. It will even be worse: Poverty, war and illiteracy will continue to threaten Nuaga till eternity. What is the cause? The way you rule offends God. Tyranny, oppression and suppression have drew the ire of Almighty to the most unbearable. Dangers ahead. Doom in sight. What is the remedy? Only appeasement and supplication in the name of Democracy. I have spoken. You may incarcerate me after this. you may kill me. But I am a voice, when gagged in one way. Raise another, louder.

GENERAL: (Intercepts his speech) vamoose out of her, you scum or your mouth land you in trouble.

ORACLE: General Ilyasu, I will bear the trouble, at least for the peace of the land. I advise you relinquish power immediately. Your Goebbels, Chukwuma whom you choose to propaganda your heinous agenda is your most undoing. Drum of lies only prepare mournful swansong of the drummer himself. That is the massage I bring from

MAJOR ADABA: the one who creates me, you and all (walks briskly out).

That wretched is a reckless mouth. something must be done about him. Must not be left to witness the appearance of coming dawn lest we risk the success of our endless transition at his dangerous expense.

GENERAL: Leave him. Soon he will curse the day he was born. Voice he calls himself?

SCENE 2

HUT OF THE ORACLE: Hunged on the wall are skin-bag containing occult and allied objects, consecrated cow-horn etc.

ORACLE: (Casts divination beads on the floor) Opele! You've said it. God at my back... On my front. Who then can I fear! (Re-cast it) You've not forgotten to remind me. Neither have I failed to remind myself.... That I hold the sacred custody of Nuaga's Eye and Mouth (Major Adaba booted the hut-door open, surveys the room and Oracle, critically. Closes in on Oracle and hit him on the head with the cudgel in his hands).

ORACLE: (Crying) Yeh! Ah! Yeh! Ah! What have I done wrong, Major?

MAJOR:	You shall know.
ORACLE:	(Crying still) what….what is my offence
MAJOR:	You soon shall know
ORACLE:	My God intercede for me
MAJOR:	Ask God to seal your mouth instead
ORACLE:	My God… My…
MAJOR:	Pray He heal that mouth. which raves in criticism. And changes your insanity. To the only same thing- how to praise.
ORACLE:	I am not a sycophant. I did not come to give underserved praise. I have come to speak the truth. (Major ransacks the hut and makes away with the objects hung on the wall).

(PRIVATE HOUSE OF GENERAL ILYASU)

GENERAL:	Welcome, Adaba. How well executed, my order?
MAJOR:	Thoroughly carried out, sir. As if it was a rebellion I was crushing. I released the most ruthless, merciless and destructive volley of bashing on the scum.

GENERAL:	And how has he taken it?
MAJOR:	Cool and calm. He has learnt his lessons, that hard way…
GENERAL:	Any sign of further mis-behaviour?
MAJOR:	None that I can notice
GENERAL:	Call Dr. Chukwuma for me
MAJOR:	He will come right now, sir (Runs out)
GENERAL:	(In deep thought) I know what I shall do. Everybody in this land of Nuaga must be brought to his knee. So that voice of dissent will not obviate our smoother plot. The way to do this is very easy, I know. At least hundreds of armoured tanks and mines, thousand of artilleries and grenades will do. But we must not lend ourselves to open suspicion that way. The land should be run down peace-meal. And unnoticeable. (Hazards a few thought) we must crush them indirectly. By some vulnerable instruments they themselves rever… (Major and Dr. Enter)

The two of you. Something just come to my mind now. That we have to haste our agenda. If not it may be unsuccessful and distrusted. Major! First thing draft our decrees, set up tribunals, its members must be our boys, you know. Let Dr. collaborates and corroborates your assignment. His campaign forceful and compelling like attack in the field of battle.

SCENE 3

THE ORACLE'S HUT

ORACLE: He who beats oracle beats God. For have not sent myself. It was God who sent me. And he who attempt to gag God's message must fall down. To the lowest of the low. Never to stand on his two feet again. Many think God is sleeping. But He is awake; only looking and watching (Pause).
I am not cursing. I have no enemy. Neither have I presented myself as one to any. I am only in the duty of the Divine. Still some have brought themselves to contravene His Law by descending on me, an infringement which attracts penalty.

(SIGH)

Just now I hear another maneuver. This time, dangerous enough to paralyze the whole land.

Thence I go to speak out divinely mandated as it were, my duty against the fashioner of terror and breeder of darkness.

The private room of the General, with him Major and Dr. Oracle enter).

MAJOR:	What are you up to, again, Oracle?
ORACLE:	(Voice loud) On a mission yet on truth Dr. Truth?
ORACLE:	Yes, truth. Over which I remain very much undaunted.
MAJOR:	So you can still make mouth, with all that fire…
ORACLE:	Fire? Bring your hell even.
MAJOR:	You will loose your life, this Big Mouth.
ORACLE:	Mmm…me? I, oracle, the Iron Coat
MAJORS:	This will serve further to destroy you

ORACLE: Can it? Are you not aware I am a salamander

MAJOR: Eh, when the hell is ultimately released…..

ORACLE: I will live through it- I am the phoenix of sprouting truth.

DR. O. K. Mr. Big Mouth, please leave here, for your own good

ORACLE: I will leave, your Honourable Goebbels of the General himself. But these plots, those Agenda bring progress to a close. Retrograde on course- poverty, war and illiteracy (Leaves).

GENERAL: (Charges at once) major? Dr?

BOTH: (Chorus) Sir.

GENERAL: Why argue…You've bandit enough unnecessary words with that stupid of a thing. Major, command five battle ready troops to descend on the foolish bug. Dr. campaign commences immediately.

SCENE 4

Five armed-Soldiers trail gun at Oracle's hut. A voice upstage commands one, two, three..
Deafening sound of gun blast rent the air as the entire hut is over-whelmed by smoke.

ACT 3

SCENE 1

On the platform Dr. addressing a large gathering.

DR. People of Nuaga, His Excellency, General Abu Ilyasu. **OPO, FGJB, RKB** wishes you good health and long life. He is assuring you that the Transition is on course. And small time now, power will reside not in him any more, but in you; the good people of Nuaga. Everyone shall have authority and power of Great Nuaga unto himself. To the left. No, to the right.

In that way, individual will direct the land to whichever way he chooses. Promises you all, will not stay a second longer beyond schedule.

(Looks over his shoulder)

I can see somebody raising up his hand to ask question (A voice) Yes, yes sir, it's me.

DR.	Let him come forward (Chief Abika wades through the crowd)

CHIEF ABIKA: I am Chief Abika- The politician. I am here today on the mandate of all the politicians of Nuaga. On their behalf I stand to ask our government the time of election that is so much brought to our hearing in news. We want to now know in the specific and with precision the very day of the election. In the same way we seek to know time table for the Transition Programme.

DR. We thank Chief Abika and all the rest politicians for their commitment.
About the day, it is any day His Excellency chooses.

CHIEF ABIKA: Which is tomorrow? Tomorrow never ends in tomorrow

DR. Tomorrow is tomorrow. Chief. Take it cool

CHIEF ABIKA: It is cool with me, Dr. But this "Tomorrow" we hear it. Time and again.

DR: It is tomorrow, Abika, I tell you. His Excellency is too big to go back on his words

CHIEF ABIKA: We know that. Dr. we are not neophytes in politicos.

DR: Everybody knows

CHIEF ABIKA: Sincerity, all we demand for

DR: Chief, what are you trying to say?

CHIEF ABIKA: I mean every military take-over subsequent promises of disengagement have not been sincere enough. We hear too often: Transition Tomorrow.

DR: Should we then say today when it is not?

CHIEF ABIKA: As you please, Dr. what, am saying is your tomorrow never end in tomorrow. (Crowd sing: Election tomorrow is another tomorrow).

CHIEF ABIKA: Another fear, Dr. if indeed tomorrow comes, the general may bring his gun as usual and goad us out of office, on the flimsiest excuse….

DR: Be assured this time. He is not interested in sitting tight….. talk less of staging a come back…..

CHIEF ABIKA: Besides. He can suddenly change like chameleon to

	wear another toga of power-khaki to civics.
DR:	Not His Excellency I know
CHIEF ABIKA:	Again fear of annulment of the election, if it ever take place.
DR:	Chief, entertain none. Governance is yours.

SCENE 2

THE STATE HOUSE

MAJOR: Sir, that goblin of oracle has been descended upon and is dead.

GENERAL: (ecstasied) spare him not even a bullet

MAJOR: Not even one, Sir. All sank deep into his flesh.

GENERAL: Good. So that Nuaga may not find out from examination who the killer is.

MAJOR: What examination, Sir?

GENERAL: Post-mortem. To discover the nature and source of death. (Oracle appears, General and Major are agape)

ORACLE: The oracle is never to be gagged. Lest be killed. I am alive. I say still bid a true final far well to force rule. Without that I see Nuaga in perpetual

GENERAL: darkness-poverty, war and illiteracy (Disappears) (angered) Liar, you are, tell me you kill...

MAJOR: I did, sir, I was surprised when...

GENERAL: Be flabbergast, even. O.K. forget that one, final assignment.

MAJOR: Very well, sir.

GENERAL: It is going to end all this trouble. Once and for all (knocks). Who is that? Come in right away. (Chief Abika enters) Ah: Chief, how are you.

CHIEF ABIKA: Fine, sir.

GENERAL: Hope no problem?

CHIEF ABIKA: Not at all, sir. It is about this handing-over.

GENERAL: Very well in place. As promised.

CHIEF ABIKA: I know. It is the only thing I trust on earth

GENERAL: I tell you. We are committed. I have always said it.

CHIEF ABIKA: However, the way Dr. riddles us in glib this morning gives rooms for doubt.

GENERAL: Glib?

CHIEF ABIKA: Something like that. Even the gathering too were confounded about it.

GENERAL: Confounded.

CHIEF ABIKA: Yes, sir. Not that he didn't present us your credible programmes. But the way he went about it…

GENERAL: Brings doubt?

CHIEF ABIKA: Exactly!

GENERAL: Don't mind, Abika. We will look into that.

CHIEF ABIKA: Good day, sir that is what I have come to tell Your Excellency (Leaves)

GENERAL: (To major) These politicians' jokes are too expensive. To expect us leave power to them as if it is a thing bought in market place. Poor power-seekers of no mean stupidity.

MAJOR: We rather be fast about it. Sir

GENERAL: It is true

MAJOR: The way I see these people. And Nuaga itself. They are not taking things easy.

GENERAL: So, see me at home tomorrow. To brief you on the final onslaught.

MAJOR: That is better, sir. (As major leaves, the delegation comes in, on another visit).

WOOD: Good day, General.

GENERAL: The same to you, our friends.

WOOD: We are happy to visit you once again.

GENERAL: So do I. You are welcome

WOOD: Sir, our president says he hasn't seen any green light….

GENERAL: My friends, it may look like that. Probably your country's official matters might well be your president's blur. Or the nerve-racking load at dark tunnel we are passing through. Surely there would be light at the end of the tunnel.

WOOD: We can't grasp the point sir.

GENERAL: I mean we need time….

WOOD: You mean to say it is a matter of time, sir?

GENERAL: Not really. After all, the handling over is tomorrow

WOOD: But our president keeps complaining…so much that he says something must be up your sleeves.

GENERAL: Nothing at all, our friends. Explain to my good friend he has every reason to believe in our word which is our bound.

SCENE 3

THE PRIVATE HOUSE OF GENERAL

GENERAL: Heh' how time flies Yesterday is gone, today is the tomorrow we've been talking about. A decisive day that I would have love to be expunged from calendar of time. I have not had a sound sleep through the night. (Major knocks and enters).

MAJOR: Good morning, sir. How was your sleep last night?

GENERAL: Disturbed all night long. This handing over trouble.

MAJOR: What about the briefing you said?

GENERAL: It is about this final onslaught we planned. With immediate dispatch, see to it that notorious parrot called oracle is imprisoned for life, all,

Chief Abika and politicians be threatened and hurled to exile. Finally, all dissents be silenced (Knocks Dr. comes in).

GENERAL: At the nick of time you came. Dr. I have just ordered imprisonment of oracle, exile of Abika and co and all oppositions to be hushed to silence. It is on your own hand how you are going to make all the loudspeakers so that the populace don't resent.

DR: It will all be carry out. More than what your Excellency could even imagine. I am prepared to lay down my life for it.

ON THE PLATFORM

DR: Good people of Nuaga. The other time I mounted this rostrum there were questions? On matter of transition. At the end, many hands were raised in our praise. Thus propping our efforts in every way. Despite, some either ignorantly or deliberately jeers at this administration sincerity. By calling it glib. These people, unknown to us are reckless usurper pointing to overthrow our ongoing transition programme.

In that way, these people rebel, insurgent, and insubordinate against authority. And success of what you great people have been yearning for-democracy. They are however reprised with deserving punishment. As a result we want you to maintain an understandable co-operation. Though today is handing over, look out till evening. The day is not closed yet.

SCENE 4

IN PRISON, ORACLE BEHIND BAR

ORACLE: I oracle of Nuaga, do I deserve this faith; a prisoner of consciences incarcerated for a service towards the betterment of the land. Bruised by incursion of gun wielders who plunged the land into unseeingly redeemable disaster. Chaos in the name of Poverty, war and illiteracy. A land innocent but battered by false messiahs. A land fresh like morning dew but scorched by self-fashioned saviours. A land flourishing but floundered by self-appointed christs. My incineration I know is temporary. Truth will sprout anew from its battered bed of silence.

THE END

www.ingramcontent.com/pod-product-compliance
Lightning Source LLC
Chambersburg PA
CBHW021041180526
45163CB00005B/2226